To:_____

From:_____

Date:_____

RICK WARREN

The Purpose Driven Life

100 Illustrated Devotions FOR Children

ILLUSTRATED BY
Morgan Huff

ZONDER**kidz**

ZONDERKIDZ

The Purpose Driven Life 100 Illustrated Devotions for Children

Copyright © 2019 by Rick Warren

Illustrations © 2019 by Morgan Huff

Requests for information should be addressed to:
Zonderkidz, 3900 Sparks Dr. SE, Grand Rapids, Michigan 49546

Library of Congress Cataloging-in-Publication Data

ISBN 978-0-310-76674-2

Art direction: Ron Huizinga

Interior design: Matthew VanZomeren

Printed in China

19 20 21 22 23   /LSC/   10 9 8 7 6 5 4 3 2 1

Introduction

This book is special just for you. It will tell you all about God's love for you and how he made you to be super special. There's nobody else in the world just like you.

As you read this book, you'll find out that God made you to make a difference in the world. Yes, you can make a difference! It doesn't matter how young you are. God has an exciting plan for you and he is going to help you every step of the way. He does this because he loves you more than you can ever know.

Have you ever put a puzzle together? It would be pretty hard to do if you didn't know what the puzzle was supposed to look like. Wouldn't it be easier if you could see a picture of the puzzle all put together?

Your life is a little like a puzzle. God made you with a lot of different pieces to your life. He gave you your very own talents and abilities. He knows what the big picture of your life looks like and he wants to help you fit the pieces together just right. Then you'll see his plan for your life. Imagine that! The God of the Universe has big plans for you. So get ready for a great adventure!

DAY 1

Anything is Possible

The sun stopped in the middle of the sky and delayed going down about a full day. There has never been a day like it before or since, a day when the LORD listened to a human being. Surely the LORD was fighting for Israel!

Joshua 10:13–14 NIV

Every day the sun comes up. Every day the sun goes down. That's because the earth rotates so the entire earth gets some sun. If the earth stopped moving, it would always be night on one side of the world. And it would always be daytime on the other side. Can you imagine playing in the dark all the time? Or going to bed with the sun still shining through your windows?

Once, God stopped the earth for a man named Joshua. Joshua needed an extra-long day to defeat his enemies and so God provided that. The Bible is full of amazing stories like this. And they

-6-

are all true! God can stop planets, move oceans, make animals talk, and change the heart of any person. With God, anything is possible.

⸙ **PRAYER** ⸙

God, I've never seen a miracle or an amazing work like those you did for people in the Bible. But I believe you can do anything.

He's Got Love
for That

*As a father has compassion on his children, so the L*ORD

has compassion on those who fear him; for he knows

how we are formed, he remembers that we are dust.

Psalm 103:13–14 NIV

God knows you inside and out—from your beating heart to every hair on top of your head. And when you make a mistake, God doesn't shake his head and wonder, "What happened with this one? I thought I did a better job."

God knows that you are not perfect. He knows that sometimes you mess up. He also knows that people can be mean and hurt your feelings. But God is always there for you. His heart is big, and his love is strong. That doesn't change because of what you do or what happens to you. God knows everything about your life. And he shows his love and kindness for you each and every day.

⊰⊱ PRAYER ⊰⊱

God, I need you. I need you when I mess up, I need you when I'm hurt, and I need you when everything is just fine. Thank you for being a good Father.

Born Right on Time

You know me inside and out, you know every bone in my body; You know exactly how I was made, bit by bit, how I was sculpted from nothing into something.

Psalm 139:15 MSG

You are here because God wanted to create you! He knew everything about you before you were even born. God chose every single part of you, from the color of your eyes to the sound of your voice. He even decided how tall you will become! He made your body just the way he wanted it. No one else is the same as you.

God made you for a reason. He made a special plan for your life that no one else has. Every day when you wake up remember—you are exactly the way you are supposed to be!

ꙅ PRAYER ꙸ

Thank you, God, for creating me. When I forget how special
I am to you, remind me that you made me just right.

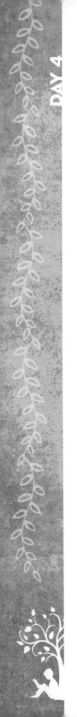

You-Nique

You saw me before I was born and scheduled

each day of my life before I began to breathe.

Every day was recorded in your book!

Psalm 139:16 TLB

God had a plan when he created you. God knew that your mom and dad were just right to create the "you" he had in mind.

God also planned where you'd be born and where you'd live. Whether you live with your parents or are adopted into a new family, that's all a part of God's big plan! Not a single thing about you was a mistake. God planned it all for his purpose.

⋙ PRAYER ⋘

God, you created me, and you don't make mistakes.
Thank you for including me as part of your purpose.

Out of This World

Long before he laid down earth's foundations, he

had us in mind, had settled on us as the focus of

his love, to be made whole and holy by his love.

Ephesians 1:4 The Message

God made everything for a reason. He made every tree and flower. He made every rabbit and rhinoceros. He made the oceans and the mountains. God made everything just as he wanted it to be. He had a big plan in mind!

God made you too. He was thinking of you even before he made the big, beautiful world. In fact, that's why he created the world. God made the world just so we could live here. The earth was made for us. And we were made for God. This is how much God loves us.

✣ PRAYER ✣

God, you made a beautiful world for me to live in. Help me to remember how much you love me whenever I look at the trees and flowers, and even when I see a rhinoceros.

Awesome Love

He who created the heavens, he is God . . . he did not

create it to be empty, but formed it to be inhabited.

Isaiah 45:18 NIV

Why did God make the whole wide world for us? Because he loves us! God's love for us is so big and wonderful—bigger and more wonderful than you can imagine!

Why did God make you? God made you because he wanted to love you. God loved you even before you were born. He loved you when you were a little baby, and he loves you right now. And he will still love you when you grow up. He will take care of you every day for the rest of your life.

God made you just so he could love you. What do you think about that?

❊ᵢᵢᵢ PRAYER ᵢᵢᵢ❊

God, thank you for showing me your awesome love.
Thank you for promising to love me forever.

Spark Your Creativity

In the beginning God created the heavens and the earth.

Genesis 1:1 NIV

God has big ideas. The whole world is full of God's big and wonderful ideas! God made big animals and small animals. He made fast animals like cheetahs, and slow animals like turtles. He made the trees and the mountains and the rivers. All of it is his. Every time you eat a peanut butter sandwich or a juicy apple, you're tasting God's wonderful ideas.

When God made people, he wanted them to have lots of ideas too. When you draw a picture, build a fort, tell a story, or think of a fun game, that's because you were created in his image and have good ideas like God does! What other big ideas do you have?

ꕥ— PRAYER —ꕥ

*God, thank you for the big ideas you give me. I
want to make amazing things for you.*

Who Jesus Is

Once when Jesus was praying in private and his disciples were with him, he asked them, "Who do the crowds say I am?" They replied, "Some say John the Baptist; others say Elijah; and still others, that one of the prophets of long ago has come back to life." "But what about you?" he asked. "Who do you say I am?"

Luke 9:18–20 NIV

Who is Jesus? A lot of people don't know the answer to that question. Some people say Jesus was just a nice guy. Other people think Jesus was a great teacher who taught people good lessons. Still others say Jesus wasn't even a real person, that he is just a character in a story.

The truth is Jesus is not only real, he is God's Son. Jesus came to earth to help us know God and to show us how he wants us to live. If we love Jesus with all our heart, we will be with him in

heaven forever. We'll also be able to share his love with others.
Loving and knowing Jesus changes everything!

PRAYER

*Jesus, I believe you are God's Son. You love us so much that you
came to earth to give us a way to join you forever. Thank you!*

A Father's Love

*And the Holy Spirit descended on him in bodily form
like a dove. And a voice came from heaven: "You are
my Son, whom I love; with you I am well pleased."*

Luke 3:22 NIV

"I love you." Those three words make you feel special. Maybe your mom or dad tell you they love you. Maybe your grandparents tell you they love you. When you know someone loves you, it makes you feel like you can do anything.

Jesus had a big job to do. He needed to go around the country teaching and healing all kinds of people. God the Father knew what Jesus needed to hear. So God spoke to Jesus from heaven. He said, "I love you. I am proud of you."

Guess what? God says these same words to you! God is proud of you. God loves you very much, and he always will.

·))) **PRAYER** (((·

Lord, I believe you love me as much as the Bible says
you do. Please help me never to forget that.

Secret Plans

On coming to the house, they saw the child with his mother Mary, and they bowed down and worshiped him. Then they opened their treasures and presented him with gifts of gold, frankincense and myrrh.

Matthew 2:11 NIV

A long time ago, God's Son, Jesus, came to earth. God let some wise men know that Jesus was coming, and the wise men took a long trip to meet Jesus.

The wise men were excited to meet Jesus and give him gifts. As soon as they saw the baby Jesus, the wise men knew he was God's Son. But not everyone knew this secret. For many years, only a few people knew that Jesus was God's Son. No one knew all the wonderful things he would do.

God doesn't always tell people about his plans. But when you wait and see what special things he is doing, you will be amazed!

❧ PRAYER ❧

God, thank you for sending Jesus to tell us about you.
Thank you for all the wonderful things you do.

Light the Darkness

In him [Jesus] was life, and that life was the light

of all mankind. The light shines in the darkness,

and the darkness has not overcome it.

John 1:4–5 NIV

Ask your mom or dad to try something with you. Find a flashlight and go to a room that you can make really, really dark. Shut the curtains and doors and put pillows or towels in front of any cracks. It has to be completely black. After a few minutes, turn on the flashlight. Look at how bright it is! The darkness makes the little light seem to shine even stronger.

Did you know Jesus called himself the light of the world? He outshines everything. Wherever Jesus goes, he shines a light. When you follow Jesus, he shines a light to guide your way—just like a flashlight in a dark room.

═╫╫═ **PRAYER** ╫╫═

Jesus, light is powerful. It helps me see my clothes, what's on my plate at dinner, and where to walk. Your light is even more powerful. Thank you for being the light in my world.

Pitch In

You are worthy, our Lord and God, to

receive glory and honor and power.

Revelation 4:11 NIV

B irds make God happy by flying, chirping, and making nests. Those are the things God made them to do. Even ants make God happy when they build their anthills and gather food. God made ants to be ants, and he made you to be you.

How can you make God happy? Here are five ways:

1. You please God by believing in him.
2. You please God by loving others.
3. You please God when you try to think, feel, and act like him.
4. You please God by helping others.
5. You please God by telling others about him.

 **PRAYER**

God, help me remember that you made me to be
me! I want my life to make you happy.

DAY 13

Count on Him

Your word, LORD, is eternal; it stands firm in the heavens. Your faithfulness continues through all generations; you established the earth, and it endures.

Psalm 119:89–90 NIV

Forever is a long time. If you try to think about how long forever is, you might get a headache. But God is forever. He's been around longer than your parents, your grandparents, or the oldest person you know. He was around before the earth was even made. In fact, he's always been around. And he has never, ever changed! He is always the same perfect God.

God will help you the same way he has helped your parents, your grandparents, and even Adam and Eve. When bad things happen or when you feel confused, remember that God wants to help you. He is always with you, and he always will be—forever!

⊰⊰⊰ **PRAYER** ⊱⊱⊱

Thank you, Lord, for never changing. Thank you for always being with me and always helping me.

Perfect Every Time

He is the Rock, his works are perfect, and all his

ways are just. A faithful God who does no wrong.

Deuteronomy 32:4 NIV

Everyone makes mistakes. No one is perfect. I make mistakes. You make mistakes. But guess what? God never makes a mistake. He never has to say, "Oops!"

That means he didn't make a mistake when he created you! Every single person is God's perfect creation, including you. God has a plan for each and every one of us. And God has a plan for you too! He made you for a reason.

ꕥ— PRAYER —ꕥ

God, you made a plan for my life. Help me remember that
you are perfect and you love me just the way I am.

Mama Bird

He will cover you with his feathers, and under

his wings you will find refuge; his faithfulness

will be your shield and rampart.

Psalm 91:4 NIV

You've probably heard that you should never touch a nest, egg, or baby chick, since the mama bird will be able to smell you and she might ignore her babies. Birds do many things to keep their eggs and chicks safe. One bird in Africa uses its spit to make its nest very strong. It doesn't want the eggs to fall out. Another bird builds such a huge nest for its babies that other birds come over to use it too. These birds really care for their families.

God loves you just like this. He watches over you with great care, like a mama bird. He takes care of your needs. He keeps his family safe. God loves you so much.

-))) **PRAYER** (((-

Thank you, Lord, for keeping me safe and taking care of me.

Crack Up

Sarah said, "God has brought me laughter, and

everyone who hears about this will laugh with me."

Genesis 21:6 NIV

What makes you laugh? Your brother or sister? Your dad? A silly cartoon? Have you ever laughed so hard you felt like you couldn't stop?

In the Bible, Sarah laughed when God surprised her with a baby boy. She was so happy. The Bible has many stories about people laughing. That's because God made laughter! He made you so you laugh when something is funny or when you feel happy or surprised. Laughter is like medicine—it makes you feel better. What a great gift from God! How can you help your friends or family laugh?

God, when my friends or family are sad, I'd like to help them laugh. Will you give me ideas to help them feel happy?

An Awesome Friend

What, then, shall we say in response to these

things? If God is for us, who can be against us?

He who did not spare his own Son, but gave

him up for us all—how will he not also, along

with him, graciously give us all things?

Romans 8:31–32 NIV

How great would it be to be friends with Mickey and Minnie Mouse and all their pals? Or your favorite superheroes? It's great to have good friends. The right kinds of friends make you feel safe and happy. They look out for you, and you can always count on them.

Well, don't you know that you've got the best friend of all on your side? God is always there for you. He even sent his Son, Jesus Christ, to earth to be your friend. And God wants you

to come live with him in heaven one day. Now that is the best friendship of all!

·»)· **PRAYER** ·«(·

*Lord, thank you for your friendship and
for always being there for me.*

BFFs

Friendship with God is reserved for those

who reverence him. With them alone he

shares the secrets of his promises.

Psalm 25:14 TLB

Everyone wants a best friend—someone to talk to and play with. You may have a best friend or even a few best friends. You'll find best friends who live near you, or maybe you'll meet them at a play date or the swimming pool. When you move to a new town, a neighbor could become your new best friend.

Did you know there is someone who can be your best friend for the rest of your life? God calls some people his friends. You can be God's friend too! Tell God you want to be friends with Jesus and ask God to be close to you. He will be the best friend you could have. And he will never, ever stop being your friend.

⇾⇾⇾ PRAYER ⇽⇽⇽

Jesus, I want you to be my best friend. Being friends with you sounds like the greatest.

He Gets a Kick Out of You

The Lord directs the steps of the godly. He

delights in every detail of their lives.

Psalm 37:23 NLT

God likes to watch everything you do. He likes watching you play, eat, and sleep. He smiles when he sees you jump, run, or spin. He doesn't miss a single move you make. That's how much he loves you.

God also likes to see you enjoy the world he made. He gave you eyes to see a pretty tree, ears to hear a sweet song, and your taste buds to enjoy a tasty treat. And you can make God happy so many different ways! When you do your chores, build a fort, play a game, or help your parents with a happy heart, it makes God happy too.

·))) ─ **PRAYER** ─ (((·

Lord, help me remember that I make you happy. And please remind
me to thank you more often for the big and little things in my life.

Feel Good for God

For the LORD takes delight in his people.

Psalm 149:4 NLT

God gave you five senses, and he gave you feelings. Why? So you can enjoy things! This is one of God's great gifts to you. He wants you to enjoy what you see, hear, taste, smell, and touch. The reason you can feel happy, have fun, and laugh is that God made you that way.

When you enjoy life, it makes God glad. You are a child of God, and you make him happy like nothing else in the whole world. The Bible says, "Because of his love, God had already decided to make us his own children through Jesus Christ. That was what he wanted and what pleased him." (Ephesians 1:5 NCV)

God, thank you for all the gifts you give me. I want to make you glad and enjoy your wonderful world.

Have You Noticed

Many, Lord my God, are the wonders you have done, the things you planned for us. None can compare with you; were I to speak and tell of your deeds, they would be too many to declare.

Psalm 40:5 NIV

God does really big, amazing things, like parting the Red Sea and raising Jesus from the dead. But did you know he also cares about little things too? He'll do sweet, little things for you in the middle of your day. He shines the sun on you. He brings you a birdsong in your backyard. It's all from God!

The big things matter. But God also wants you to see those little things he does for you. When you see those little things, tell others. Talk about all the good things that God does for you. That will help other people learn to see him too!

Lord, help me see your love today. And show me all the little things you do for me. Thank you for loving me so much.

Music Makers

Clap your hands, all you nations; shout to God

with cries of joy. Sing praises to God, sing

praises; sing praises to our King, sing praises.

Psalm 47:1, 6 NIV

The oldest known musical instrument in the world is a type of flute. It was made many thousands of years ago. That means people made music and probably danced way back then! The people who lived during the Bible times loved music too. They played all sorts of instruments, and they liked to make up songs.

Music is a wonderful gift from God. That's why people sing at church. Even the angels in heaven make music for God. So if you love music or love playing an instrument, keep it up. Singing brings joy to other people and to God.

DAY 22

ꙮ PRAYER ꙮ

*Lord, thank you for making music. I want all my
singing and music-making to bring you joy!*

Need a Boost?

For physical training is of some value, but

godliness has value for all things, holding promise

for both the present life and the life to come.

1 Timothy 4:8 NIV

"**E**at your vegetables!" How many times have you heard that? Why do your parents or babysitters tell you that? Because when you eat veggies, they give you vitamins and lots of other stuff that's good for your body. Getting up and moving around is good for your body too.

Want to know another thing that's good for you? Getting to know God! Knowing God helps you to have a healthy, happy life right now, and later when you grow up. Getting to know God is good for your mind and your heart. Try to spend time with God each day.

Lord, I want to get to know you. I know it is good for me, just like eating healthy and being active. Will you help my body, mind, and heart grow strong?

Stronger than Fear

Fearing people is a dangerous trap, but

trusting the LORD means safety.

Proverbs 29:25 NLT

Count how many things you are afraid of. It's normal to feel afraid of the dark, snakes, bugs, and the woods. The world has lots of scary things in it. But God wants to help you feel fearless. And you know what? He can.

It's not fun to be hurt, so it's normal to be scared of things that might hurt you. But God can help you. He can make you brave like him. He can make you so strong inside that you won't feel so afraid of things on the outside. After all, God made the whole world, so he's not afraid of anything in it. Even the dark or creepy creatures don't scare our great big God.

Lord, I am afraid of [fill in the blank]. But you aren't afraid of those
things. Thank you for keeping me safe and helping me be brave.

DAY 25

Secret Keeper

I have hidden your word in my heart,

that I might not sin against you.

Psalm 119:11 NLT

Think about your friends. Who is your best friend? What do you like about that person?

Job and David were God's good friends. Know why? They believed what God told them with their whole hearts. And they thought about it over and over. They knew God well, so God became their friend.

Friends trust and care for each other. They also share secrets. It's true—God will share his secrets with you if you get to know him, just like Job and David. He wants to be that close to you. Are you ready for a new best friend?

PRAYER

God, it sounds really cool to be your best friend. Please show me how to be friends with you and learn more about you.

Happy to Obey

I have loved you even as the Father has loved me. Live

within my love. When you obey me you are living

in my love, just as I obey my Father and live in his

love. I have told you this so that you will be filled

with my joy. Yes, your cup of joy will overflow!

John 15:9–11 TLB

Look at what Jesus said in John 15. Jesus obeyed his Father, and he wants us to obey him too. Jesus loved God the Father, so Jesus did whatever the Father asked him to do—no questions asked.

Love is the reason God created us. Love is the reason Jesus came to earth. Love is the reason Jesus forgives our sins. It only makes sense that we do what he says, because he is so loving to us. He always knows what is best. And obeying Jesus is a wonderful way to show how much we love him!

⋙ **PRAYER** ⋘

*Jesus, I want to be friends with you. Thank you for loving me
so much. I want to obey you and follow where God leads me.*

What Are You Afraid Of?

Where God's love is, there is no fear, because

God's perfect love drives out fear.

1 John 4:18 NCV

Do you ever feel afraid of the dark? Or of being made fun of? Or of being hurt? There are hundreds of scary things that can make you feel afraid.

Lots of kids—and adults—let fear take over their lives. Some fears can help keep you safe, like staying away from a snake or the edge of a cliff. But fear of trying something new, telling the truth, or doing something difficult will keep you from doing everything God wants you to do. Want to know the best way to fight fear? Trust in God and his love!

⫸ **PRAYER** ⫷

God, help me to be brave. I know that you love and care
for me. I want to be everything you created me to be.

Hand Them Over

This is what the LORD says—your Redeemer,

who formed you in the womb: I am the LORD,

the Maker of all things, who stretches out the

heavens, who spreads out the earth by myself.

Isaiah 44:24 NIV

Many problems in the world are very big. You might wonder how God can help families who don't have enough to eat, or all the people who are sick. Such big problems seem too hard to fix. Can God really do anything about all of them?

God likes to remind us how big he is. Remember that God made each and every person on earth—that's more than seven billion people! If that doesn't seem like a big enough God, then look at all the stars and the planets that fill the night sky. He made all those too!

Nothing is too big for our God to handle. He is bigger than every problem—so you can tell him about everything that worries you.

—}}}— **PRAYER** —{{{—

Lord, help me remember that there is nothing
too big for you to handle. Thank you!

Call Him Up

I cry aloud to the LORD, and he answers

me from his holy mountain.

Psalm 3:4 CSB

G od sees and hears everything. Even if a million people
are praying all at the same time, he hears each one.
You can talk to God any time. He wants to hear from
you. He wants to know when you are happy, when you're sad,
and about anything you're thinking. He likes to spend time with
you, because he is your friend. Each time you talk to God, he gets
closer to you. It's like he says, "I was just waiting to come over to
see you. Thanks for calling."

-))) — **PRAYER** — (((-

Lord, thank you for hearing my prayers and the prayers
of every person on earth. I want to be close to you.

Made for Family

The Spirit we received does not make us slaves again

to fear; it makes us children of God. With that spirit

we cry out, "Father." And the Spirit himself joins

with our spirits to say we are God's children.

Romans 8:15–16 NCV

The Bible tells the story of God's family. It's a family who will love him and be with him forever. Sounds like a good family to be part of!

God doesn't get lonely like we do. He didn't create a family because he needed one. He created a family because he wanted one. God wanted to show his love to others, so he created people, including you. You were made to be in his family. He wanted you to be a part of it before you were even born. He wants to welcome you in and share all he has with you. You are his child, and he is your loving Father.

⋙ PRAYER ⋘

God, thank you for making me part of your family!
I am so glad you call me your child.

Love Everybody

All the believers were one in heart and mind. No

one claimed that any of their possessions was their

own, but they shared everything they had . . .

There were no needy persons among them.

Acts 4:32, 34 NIV

How many people do you love? Two, three, five, or maybe even ten? Just after Jesus left earth, his followers were full of love. They all loved each other, so they made sure everyone had enough to eat and a place to sleep.

God gives his love to us so we can share that love with others. When we really love others, we want to share with them and help them out. Love flows right out of us!

You can ask God to bring more people into your life to love. He will always fill you with more love to give.

✤ PRAYER ✤

Lord, will you fill my heart with love? Your true love is amazing. Please help me show that kind of love to others.

Share a Little or a Lot

All these people gave their gifts out of their wealth; but she [a poor woman] out of her poverty put in all she had to live on.

Luke 21:4 NIV

Would it be hard for you to share one cookie if you only had two? How about sharing three cookies if you had six? It seems like it would be harder to give away one cookie if it left you with only one. But what if you were sharing that cookie with your favorite person in the whole world? Would it be easier to give it away?

It's easier to share with the people you love the most. Jesus pointed out a poor woman who had almost nothing. But she loved God so much that she didn't mind giving her last coins to him. When love like this fills your heart, you can be happy to share with others too.

God, please fill my heart with love for you and for others.
And please help me share when you ask me to.

Show Me!

I am praying to you because I know you will answer, O God. Bend down and listen as I pray. Show me your unfailing love in wonderful ways. By your mighty power you rescue those who seek refuge from their enemies.

Psalm 17:6–7 NLT

David knew he could count on God. He knew God would hear his voice, and he knew that God would answer him. David wasn't afraid to ask God to show him signs of his love. Most kids don't think to ask God for things like that. But David knew how much God loved him.

God loves you too. You can see that love in a million different ways. He shows it through pretty sunsets, tall mountains, and deep blue oceans. You can feel God's love when your friend smiles at you, when someone shows you kindness, and when you laugh with people you love.

Look for the ways God shows his love for you. Then answer, "I love you too."

⟶ PRAYER ⟵

God, thank you for loving me. Thank you for showing me your love in so many different ways. I love you.

Where is the Love?

If I have the gift of prophecy and can fathom

all mysteries and all knowledge, and if

I have a faith that can move mountains,

but do not have love, I am nothing.

1 Corinthians 13:2 NIV

Think of the biggest mountain or hill around your home. Imagine walking outside one day and seeing that mountain is gone. Someone moved it from one side of town to the other. Wow! Now imagine a friend of yours had prayed a prayer, and—poof!—that's how the mountain moved.

God tells us that a person can do really amazing things just by believing in God's power. But do you know what God cares about even more than amazing miracles? Love! Love matters more than miracles, moving mountains, or doing everything right. God wants us to love him and love other people. And when we do, that's when amazing things happen. So, how can you be loving today?

God, please fill me up with love today. I want to love you and other people with all my heart.

Frenemies

If you love those who love you, what credit is that

to you? Even sinners love those who love them.

And if you do good to those who are good to you,

what credit is that to you? Even sinners do that.

Luke 6:32–33 NIV

Dealing with friends and enemies can be really tricky. Everyone loves the warm, fuzzy feelings that come from good friends. But it's hard to love someone who hurts your feelings or does something mean to you.

God wants you to love others, even when it's hard. God gives us that kind of love. God loves you on good days, and he still loves you when you make bad choices or are mean to others. God asks you to love others like that. When it feels hard to love someone, remember how much love God has for you, on good days and bad.

Lord, it's hard to love people who make me angry. Will you help me? I want to love people the way you love me.

Life of Love

By this everyone will know that you are

my disciples, if you love one another.

John 13:35 CSB

Feeling loved is one of the best things in the world. Think about who loves you: your mom or dad, a grandparent, a best friend. How do you show them love?

Love is so important to God. He's the one who created love! And being loving is the most important thing he wants you to learn how to do. When you love others, you act most like God—because God is so loving.

Sometimes it's hard to be loving. It takes practice, just like learning to ride a bike. But the more you practice, the more God will fill your heart with love.

God, I don't want to keep my love to myself. Please help me show love to everyone around me.

The Big House

But I, by your great love, can come into your house;

in reverence I bow down toward your holy temple.

Psalm 5:7 NIV

Sitting in church seems boring sometimes, doesn't it? Do you wonder why it's so important? You may not understand everything the minister says, but church is the place that God thinks of as home.

Going to church is a lot like going to visit a friend's home. In God's home, though, he wants people to come to worship him. Worship means seeing how wonderful God is and telling him. Worship can be singing songs to him, praying to him, and enjoying the other people who are there with you. Next time you go to church, remember that you're visiting God's home.

❧ **PRAYER** ❧

Lord, thanks for inviting me to your home. I want to
enjoy my visits and worship you when I'm there.

Deep and Wide

The LORD is merciful and loving, slow to become angry,

and full of constant love . . . As high as the sky is above

the earth, so great is his love for those who honor him.

Psalm 103:8, 11 GNT

The next time you are at the top of a tall building or flying in an airplane, look down to see if you can see anything on the ground. Everything below is so far away. Now imagine hiking up a mountain all the way into the clouds. You wouldn't even be halfway to the heavens. That's a long way!

God's love is that big—he loves and he loves and he loves. The next time you look up to the sky or down from a plane, thank God for his great big love.

✤ PRAYER ✤

*God, thank you for your big, amazing love for me and
for everyone in the world. I don't really understand
it, but I want to feel it and show it to others.*

God's House

Better is one day in your courts than a thousand

elsewhere; I would rather be a doorkeeper in the house

of my God than dwell in the tents of the wicked.

Psalm 84:10 NIV

Think about your favorite place to be or a place that you really, really want to go. Would you love to live at Disney World all the time? Maybe you want to live in Hawaii and go swimming every day.

King David had a favorite place too—he loved God's house more than anywhere else. David loved to worship and talk with God. He couldn't imagine any other place he'd rather be.

Church may not seem like your number one place, but when you remember that God lives there, Disney World won't even compare.

⚜ PRAYER ⚜

God, I want to be with you, either at church or when I'm at home talking to you. I'd like to feel the same happiness that David felt when he spent time with you.

More Fun with Others

Two are better than one, because they have a
good return for their labor: If either of them falls
down, one can help the other up. But pity anyone
who falls and has no one to help them up.

Ecclesiastes 4:9–10 NIV

L ife can be really fun when you have a friend, brother or sister, or maybe a cousin to play with, talk to, and share with. God enjoys the company of his Son Jesus and the Holy Spirit, and he likes having a relationship with you. He wants you to enjoy relationships too.

Sometimes it's good to be quiet and alone. But God made us to be around other people. He doesn't want us to be lonely. Remember that he is always with you, and if you are feeling alone, ask him to bring friends and family to you. Life is more fun when you share it with others.

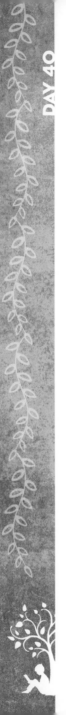

Lord, sometimes I don't want to be around people, but you've said they are important. Please show me how important other people are to my life and how I can be a good friend.

Family Resemblance

For God knew his people in advance, and he chose

them to become like his Son, so that his Son would

be the firstborn among many brothers and sisters.

Romans 8:29 NLT

Have you ever heard someone say, "Like father, like son?" When someone says my kids act or look like me it makes me happy. God feels the same way about you.

Only human beings are made to be like God. How cool! Every single person is like God in certain ways. Here are a few examples:

1. We have spirits that will live forever.
2. We can think, understand, and solve problems.
3. We can give real love and be loved by others.
4. We can know right from wrong.

As you grow up, God will be happy to see all the ways you are like him.

PRAYER

God, I'm glad you made me to be like you. Thank you for making me. Please help me grow to become even more like you every day.

Slowly, Slowly

This will continue until we all come to such

unity in our faith and knowledge of God's Son

that we will be mature in the Lord, measuring up

to the full and complete standard of Christ.

Ephesians 4:13 NLT

You are a masterpiece—but you're not finished yet! It takes years and years to grow up. You'll get taller. You'll get stronger. You'll get smarter. So don't worry about trying to grow up too fast. God made you to grow slowly.

Becoming like God takes time too. Even when your body is all grown up, the spirit inside of you is never finished growing. It will only be finished when you get to heaven or when Jesus returns. And when that day comes, you will become just like Jesus!

 PRAYER

Jesus, I look forward to the day when I will truly be like you.

Dreaming Big

Whatever you do in word or deed, do all in

the name of the Lord Jesus, giving thanks

through Him to God the Father.

Colossians 3:17 NASB

D o you ever think about what you want to be when you grow up? Maybe you want to be an astronaut and travel to space. Maybe you want to be a chef and cook yummy food. God will put lots of dreams for the future in your heart. And he loves it when you talk to him about your dreams. But God cares more about who you are than what you do.

God has plans for all sorts of jobs and activities in your life. But the most important thing is to be kind and good . . . just like Jesus.

ꗃ PRAYER ꕭ

Thank you, God, for caring about the little details of my life. Thank you for the dreams in my heart, and please help me to be like Jesus.

Good Things Grow

But the fruit of the Spirit is love, joy, peace, forbearance,

kindness, goodness, faithfulness, gentleness and

self-control. Against such things there is no law.

Galatians 5:22–23 NIV

Farmers grow lots of things on their farms—flowers, vegetables, fruits, and grains. These growing things need plenty of water, sunshine, and healthy soil to grow. The farmer doesn't just plant a seed and have a tall apple tree the next day. No, it takes time and special care.

Just like flowers on a farm, we take time to grow and blossom into the people God wants us to be. We don't just ask God to make us kind, good, and gentle and then—poof!—it happens. We have to wait. It's our job to do our part, but God is the farmer that helps good things grow inside our hearts.

Lord, help me do my part to grow your fruit in my heart,
by spending time with you and talking to you.

Time to Fly

God blesses those who patiently endure testing and temptation. Afterward they will receive the crown of life that God has promised to those who love him.

James 1:12 NLT

Did you know that a mama eagle will sometimes kick her children out of the nest? It's true! She does this so that they learn to fly on their own. God does this to us sometimes too. He will let us be a little unhappy so that we grow and learn.

If you are feeling bad about something right now, God may be getting ready to change you for the better. He doesn't want you to feel afraid or frustrated, but he also doesn't want you to be stuck in the nest like a baby bird. He wants to help you fly.

﹒⫸ **PRAYER** ⫷﹒

God, it's not fun feeling bad or dealing with problems.
Even though change is hard, I know you do it for my
good. Help me to trust that you will take care of me.

Anchor Yourself

I belong to God, and I worship him. Last night he sent

an angel to tell me, "Paul, don't be afraid! You will

stand trial before the Emperor. And because of you,

God will save the lives of everyone on the ship."

Acts 27:23–24 CEV

Storms can never hide us from God. We may not see him, but he sees us. We may think God is a million miles away, but he is with us and watching over us.

When Paul was in a shipwreck, God sent an angel to remind Paul he wasn't alone. God was with him, even in the middle of the storm.

The Bible says over and over that wherever we are, God is right there beside us. We never go through anything by ourselves. No matter what hard things happen in your life, remember that God is always with you.

⟩⟩⟩ ——PRAYER—— ⟨⟨⟨

God, thank you for being with me through everything.
You are the anchor that keeps me steady in any storm.

Lifeguard on Duty

When you pass through the waters, I will be

with you; and when you pass through the

rivers, they will not sweep over you.

Isaiah 43:2 NIV

Not knowing how to swim can be a little scary. If you stay in the kiddie pool where you can touch both feet to the bottom, it's okay. But if you go in the big pool, that's another story.

God knows that the swimming pool isn't the only time we feel "in over our heads." Many things in life might scare us, like getting lost or not being able to find a favorite toy. But God is like a lifeguard watching over us. Instead of worrying about the things that scare us, we should remember that he is always with us.

PRAYER

Lord, it helps to know that you are watching over me everywhere I go. I'm glad I don't have to be afraid.

The Best Hiding Spot

You are my hiding place; you will protect me from

trouble and surround me with songs of deliverance.

Psalm 32:7 NIV

Where is your favorite hiding place? Under your bed? In your closet? In the backyard? Under a big tree in the park? When you're afraid or tired of being with people, where do you go?

Everyone has a place where they go when they want to be alone. But here's an idea: go to your hiding place every day. But instead of just reading or playing, why not pray too? Thank God that he is bigger than the things that make you afraid. Thank him for being a safe place for you.

Lord, when I feel like hiding, please take care of me. You know the things that make me scared. When I run to my hiding place, will you also be my safe place?

Ow! That Hurts!

A woman giving birth to a child has pain

because her time has come; but when her baby

is born she forgets the anguish because of her

joy that a child is born into the world.

John 16:21 NIV

Has anybody ever told you that you were a real pain? Well, it's true! Just ask your mom. On the day you were born, you may have caused her quite a lot of pain. Giving birth is hard work, but you were worth it.

Jesus uses giving birth to teach us a lesson about hard times. He tells us that pain is part of life. Sometimes we have tough days, but they don't last forever. The "ouches" will turn into "yippees." And when we are patient during the hard times, our faith gets stronger and stronger.

⫸⫸⫸ **PRAYER** ⫷⫷⫷

Lord, I know my faith isn't always very strong yet.
Thank you for giving me strength when I need it.

No One Will Notice, Right?

If you hide your sins, you will not succeed. If you

confess and reject them, you will receive mercy.

Proverbs 28:13 NCV

et's pretend you don't like to eat brussels sprouts. But your mother loves them. She serves them for dinner once a week. Let's pretend that your dog loves them. What would you do? Should you be sneaky and feed yours to the dog?

Wait a minute! If your mom told you to eat them and you really didn't, that's sinful. And so is tricking her. Maybe you wouldn't get caught right away. But it hurts us inside when we keep our sins a secret. Try being honest instead. It will be a better ending than having a dog full of veggies.

PRAYER

Being honest about what I did wrong feels hard, Lord. But I don't want to hide my sin. Thank you for helping me tell the truth.

Always Good

And we know that for those who love God

all things work together for good, for those

who are called according to his purpose.

Romans 8:28 ESV

Everything in life is not always good. There are some bad things in this world. But if you follow and believe in God, God will make good come out of all things—even the bad. God is greater than any problem you will ever face, and he wants only good things for you. He will even take a yucky problem and somehow make something good come from it. When you have a problem, it can be hard to see how God could do that. But if you have faith and trust in God, one day you can see for yourself.

God, you don't promise that everything will be easy or
problem-free. But you do promise to always be with me.
Help me to trust in you even when it's hard to.

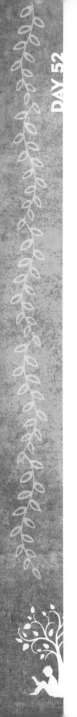

Bodies and Brains

In his hand are the depths of the earth, and the

mountain peaks belong to him. The sea is his, for

he made it, and his hands formed the dry land.

Psalm 95:4–5 NIV

People can make their bodies and brains do amazing things. Have you heard stories about people who can dunk a basketball, or flip backwards, do really hard math problems, write a book, or run for a hundred miles straight?

Our bodies and brains are incredible. But they cannot compare to God. God can climb a tall mountain, walk across a continent, dive to the bottom of the ocean, and solve the world's toughest math problems. But he did something even better—he made all those things with his amazing power and genius. Best of all, he created you too!

Lord, you are so amazing! Sometimes it's hard to believe that you made me so special and want to be friends with me. I want to be your friend too.

Cleaning Up the Inside

Then the Lord said to him, "Now then, you Pharisees clean the outside of the cup and dish, but inside you are full of greed and wickedness. You foolish people! Did not the one who made the outside make the inside also?

Luke 11:39–40 NIV

Imagine if your mom told you to go clean your room so your cousin can sleep there when she visits. Would your mom be happy if you threw a nice blanket and pretty pillows on the bed, but hid all your dirty socks under the quilt? Probably not. And neither would your cousin!

Sometimes people are like that with God. They pretend to love God on the outside. But inside, their hearts are like dirty laundry. They don't really love God at all. Jesus cares about what's inside you, not how you look on the outside. He wants to help everyone be truly loving and lovely—inside and outside.

⇾⟩⟩⟩ **PRAYER** ⟨⟨⟨⇽

Jesus, I know there are messy thoughts and feelings inside me.
You know who I really am, and you love me anyway. Please
help me clean up my heart and be loving inside and out.

Stubborn as an Ox

For I know how stubborn and obstinate you

are. Your necks are as unbending as iron.

Your heads are as hard as bronze.

Isaiah 48:4 NLT

Make your arms as stiff as possible down at your sides and press your arms into the sides of your body. Now ask a friend to try to move your arms or bend your elbows. It will be tough for them!

Stubbornness is like tightening all your muscles at once so your body won't move. Do you ever feel that way inside? What do you feel stubborn about? Cleaning your room, sharing your toys, going to church? Go ahead and tighten every muscle in your body (and stomp your feet too) to get out the stubbornness. Then loosen up and let it go.

﹏ PRAYER ﹏

God, there are some things that I just don't want to do.
Help me stop being stubborn and to do the things I should,
like serving you and doing what my parents tell me.

Remember What?

Then he adds: "Their sins and lawless acts I will remember no more." And where these have been forgiven, sacrifice for sin is no longer necessary.

Hebrews 10:17–18 NIV

God forgets. Oh, he doesn't forget us or forget what he has to do every day. But he forgets our mistakes and bad choices. The minute we ask him to forgive us, he does it. Isn't that incredible?

We remember when our friends hurt our feelings. We also remember how bad it feels when we lie or get in trouble with our parents. God knows we may have trouble forgetting, but he doesn't want us to hold on to bad feelings. If someone asks us to forgive them, you need to do it.

Since God forgives the bad stuff we do, he wants us to forgive too.

⋙ ─PRAYER─ ⋘

Lord, help me not to hold on to bad feelings when others have hurt my feelings. I want to forgive and forget them, just like you do.

Motives of the Heart

All a person's ways seem pure to them, but

motives are weighed by the LORD.

Proverbs 16:2 NIV

Most of us like to think we are good. We think, "I listen to my parents; I pick up my toys; I help my friends. So I must be a good person!"

God looks at our hearts. He knows if we are being nice and obedient out of love or if we just want to stay out of trouble. God still loves us when we do good things for the wrong reasons. But he wants to change our hearts so that he can guide us. God can show us what's really in our hearts, and he will help us do things for the best reasons.

≫—**PRAYER**—≪

Lord, look at my heart. I want to do the right thing
for the right reasons. Will you please help me?

Doing Your Part

Then have them make a sanctuary for me, and I will dwell among them. Make this tabernacle and all its furnishings exactly like the pattern I will show you.

Exodus 25:8–9 NIV

Do you love building things? Or creating colorful pieces of artwork? How would you feel if God asked you and your friends to build him a house? Well, a long time ago he asked his people to do just that.

Everyone pitched in. They gave their silver, gold, bronze, wood, and even yarn. People brought leather, stones, gems, and spices and oils to use too. God gave them all the instructions they needed. Everybody just had to do their part.

Every person has something to give God. No one is left out! You can help with God's projects too.

·))){ **PRAYER** }(((·

Lord, I want to help with your projects on earth. Will you show me my part?

Original Beauty

Bezalel made the ark of acacia wood . . . He overlaid

it with pure gold, both inside and out, and made

a gold molding around it. He cast four gold rings

for it and fastened them to its four feet, with two

rings on one side and two rings on the other.

Exodus 37:1–3 NIV

Bezalel did not have the prettiest or coolest name. But he knew how to make beautiful creations with his hands. God chose Bezalel to make a special box called an ark to keep in God's house. Bezalel spent days making sure the golden ark looked just right.

Why did God care what the ark looked like? God loves beautiful things. When he created the world, he made people, animals, plants, mountains, and lakes. He made many beautiful things in this world—including you. He's an amazing artist! And he wants you to enjoy all of his beautiful creations.

-))) **PRAYER** (((-

Lord, thank you for making beautiful things. Please show me what is beautiful about me and how I can make beautiful things for you.

Inventors Welcome

In Jerusalem [Uzziah] inventors made equipment

for shooting arrows and for throwing large stones

from the towers in corners of the city wall. His fame

spread everywhere, and he became very powerful

because of the help he received from God.

2 Chronicles 26:15 GNT

You may not think much about it but someone had to invent many of the things you use every day. Bowls for breakfast cereal. Forks and knives for dinner. Bicycles. Television. Even a potty so you don't have to go in the backyard with your dog. People come up with all sorts of helpful ideas.

That's because God created us to be creative. And some people use their creativity to invent new things. That means we can be thankful to God even for an invention like the potty.

Today, remember to thank God for all the inventions you use that make life easier.

Lord, thank you for creativity and inventions. I don't usually think about who made the inventions I use every day. But I know you are behind all of them.

Open Your Gifts

It is the same and only Holy Spirit who

gives all these gifts and powers, deciding

which each one of us should have.

1 Corinthians 12:11 TLB

God gives special gifts to every member of his family. These gifts are things we can do to serve God. You don't earn or get to choose these special gifts—that's why they are called gifts! God decides that.

God wants us all to be one-of-a-kind. So he doesn't give the same gift or talent to everyone. And no one has every talent either. That way, we can use our gifts to help each other. We all need each other—that's why God made us a family!

Ask God to show you which gifts you have.

Lord, sometimes I wish I could be good at the same things my friends are good at. Show me the special gifts you've given me and show me ways I can use them to serve you and help others.

The Perfect Age

People were bringing little children to Jesus for him to

place his hands on them, but the disciples rebuked them.

When Jesus saw this, he was indignant. He said to them,

"Let the little children come to me, and do not hinder

them, for the kingdom of God belongs to such as these."

Mark 10:13–14 NIV

How old are you? Five, six, seven, eight years old? Do you ever wish you were older? Sometimes you might think older kids seem more important, or that God cares more about adults than children. Guess what? God loves children just as much as the oldest grandma or grandpa.

Of course, you still need to respect adults! But remember that kids can do things for God too. You don't have to wait to be all grown up or smarter or stronger. When Jesus was on Earth, he told the children to visit him. He loves kids, and he never wants you to feel left out. Jesus always wants to spend time with you!

✻ PRAYER ✻

Lord, thanks for treating me as special, even though I'm a kid. Will you show me how I can do something good for you, just the way I am?

Who God Chooses

John wore clothing made of camel's hair, with a leather belt around his waist, and he ate locusts and wild honey. And this was his message: "After me comes the one more powerful than I, the straps of whose sandals I am not worthy to stoop down and untie."

Mark 1:6–7 NIV

Ever wonder why God chooses certain people to do his work? John the Baptist ran around in the desert, hair sticking out in every direction, dirty as can be. God could have picked anyone to introduce Jesus to the world. But he chose wild, stinky John the Baptist.

And John the Baptist was exactly who Jesus wanted. Jesus loved John. He even let John baptize him. If a guy who eats locusts for lunch can do good things for God, you can too.

⊰⊱ PRAYER ⊰⊱

Lord, thank you for helping me understand that I can always be myself for you. I want to be the person you created me to be. Please help me serve you with my whole heart.

Naturally You

He chose David his servant and took him from the sheep

pens; from tending the sheep he brought him to be the

shepherd of his people Jacob, of Israel his inheritance.

Psalm 78:70–71 NIV

You don't usually imagine kings and presidents working in normal, everyday places but did you know that Abraham Lincoln worked in a post office before he became president? And King David worked as a shepherd. Most people who do great things for God were just like you when they were young.

Abraham Lincoln's job taught him how to work hard. And David learned how to fight by protecting his flock from dangerous animals. What about you? You can learn to use the talents God has given you right now, while you're still a kid. Then you'll be ready when God sends you on a mission he's already planned for you.

God, I want to do great things for you. Help me to remember that and to keep my eyes on you. Show me how I can start using my talents for you right now.

Gift-Worthy

King Solomon was greater in riches and wisdom

than all the other kings of the earth. All the kings

of the earth sought audience with Solomon to

hear the wisdom God had put in his heart.

2 Chronicles 9:22–23 NIV

God doesn't want to give gifts and talents to people who will waste them. That's why he gave King Solomon so much money. Solomon didn't ask God for money. Solomon asked God for wisdom—the smarts to make good and right decisions. So God knew he could give Solomon lots of gold, because Solomon wouldn't waste it. Instead, Solomon shared his gifts with his people.

What do you think God wants to give you?

Wisdom

⁂— PRAYER —⁂

God, your wisdom is the best. Will you please give me the smarts to take care of and use your gifts now and forever?

Are You a Servant?

We should help people whenever we can,

especially if they are followers of the Lord.

Galatians 6:10 CEV

A man named John Wesley was an incredible servant, or helper, of God. He said we should help as many people as we can, everywhere we can, for as long as we can. Servants like John Wesley pay attention to what other people need. They always look for ways to help others. When you see someone in need, that means God is giving you a chance to be a helper.

Every morning, remind yourself that you are God's servant. Then start looking for small things you can do to help other people. Do these little things as if they were great things, because God is watching.

God, help me see the small things I can do to serve others.
I want to pay better attention to help people in need.

Heartbeats

Watch over your heart with all diligence,

for from it flow the springs of life.

Proverbs 4:23 NASB

Each of us has our own unique heartbeat. Think about all the people who have ever lived on Earth. No one's heartbeat has ever been exactly like yours!

The Bible uses the word "heart" to mean all the things you like, hope for, and dream about. It also means everything you love to do and the things you care about most. God made it so that your heart beats fast when you are excited about something. What things make your heart get excited? Maybe that's something you can use to serve God and other people.

PRAYER

Wow, God, you made me so unique that even my heart beats differently from every other person who ever lived! Will you show me how to use my heart to serve you and others in my own special way?

Ready to Serve

Be ready for whatever comes, dressed for action and with

your lamps lit, like servants who are waiting for their

master to come back from a wedding feast. When he

comes and knocks, they will open the door for him at once.

Luke 12:35–36 GNT

If your best friend invited you to go to bike riding with her, would you go in your pajamas? No way. You'd ask your mom or dad to help you find the right clothes and gear. You'd need sturdy shoes and a helmet. You might also want some water for when you get thirsty. Then you'd be ready!

Living for Jesus also means you need to get ready. Jesus said that he will come back to Earth one day to take all his followers to heaven. How do you get ready for something like that? Ask God to lead you each day. When you do something for God, it lets others know about him. Then maybe they will be excited for Jesus to return to Earth too—whenever that may be.

❊❊❊ PRAYER ❊❊❊

Jesus, I want to be ready when you come back to Earth. Please show me how to do that every day.

Weakness Expected

Keep falsehood and lies far from me; give me neither poverty nor riches, but give me only my daily bread. Otherwise, I may have too much and disown you and say, "Who is the LORD?" Or I may become poor and steal, and so dishonor the name of my God.

Proverbs 30:8–9 NIV

The comic book hero Superman has one weakness. A rock called kryptonite makes his powers go away. So he stays as far away from it as he can! Everyone, even Superman, has a weakness.

Do you know what your weakness is? Do you try to keep away from it? Maybe you like to keep secrets from people. Maybe you like to eat junk food a little too much. Or maybe you don't like to share what you have with others.

If you don't know your weakness, that's okay. As you grow up, you'll find out. And when you do, ask God to help you fight it.

PRAYER

Lord, show me my weakness and help me remember
I can rely on you to be my strength.

Serve First

Then James and John, the sons of Zebedee, came to him. "Teacher," they said, "we want you to do for us whatever we ask." "What do you want me to do for you?" he asked. They replied, "Let one of us sit at your right and the other at your left in your glory."

Mark 10:35–37 NIV

Two brothers in the Bible asked Jesus if they could have special favors. They wanted to be more special than everyone else. Can you believe it? They were being selfish, so Jesus decided to help them figure out what being special really means. Jesus told the brothers that being special is not about asking for favors. He said it is better to ask for ways to serve others instead.

Try looking for ways to be helpful. Choose to be kind when no one else will. God thinks it's great when you care for other people.

⫸ **PRAYER** ⫷

Lord, I like to feel special. But I want to be great in the ways that matter to you. Forgive me when I try to grab the best for myself.

Directed by a Dream

After Paul had seen the vision, we got ready at once to leave for Macedonia, concluding that God had called us to preach the gospel to them.

Acts 16:10 NIV

Have you ever imagined you were chasing down a bear or hanging off a cliff above a rushing river? We've all had thoughts that make us wonder, "Where did that come from?"

Sometimes God gives us a sense of something he wants us to do, like a picture of what we will be when we grow up. But how do you know if the idea is really from God? The best thing to do is talk to a grown-up and to see if what you are thinking is something the Bible says is acceptable. God has a way of letting you know if you're doing the right thing. He will point you in the right direction.

Lord, I want to do what you ask me to do.

Please point me in the right direction.

Use it or Lose it

God has given each of you a gift from his great variety of spiritual gifts. Use them well to serve one another.

1 Peter 4:10, NLT

When someone gives you a gift, you know the right thing to do is use it, right? The same is true of the gifts God has given to you. It makes him happy when you use your special gifts. And it makes other people happy too!

If you have a talent for singing, sing! If you have a talent for drawing, draw! If you have a talent for helping out in the kitchen, try to do that as much as you can. Your gifts may not seem like big things to you, but the little things can mean a lot. Using your gifts (big ones and little ones!) is one way of showing God that you believe in his plan for you.

God, I want to show you that I believe in your plan, not just in the big things but in the little things too. I know you will do big things if I use my special gifts.

God Always Notices

God is not unjust; he will not forget your work
and the love you have shown him as you have
helped his people and continue to help them.

Hebrews 6:10 NIV

Maybe you can't jump the highest, run the fastest, or sing like a rock star. But that doesn't mean you're not special! God sees how great you are all the time. He notices everything. He sees when you help your mom in the kitchen. He sees when you practice your reading and writing. He sees when you are kind to someone.

You probably won't get a trophy for doing these things. Sometimes other people don't even notice when you do something kind or good. But God always notices. Every time you show love to someone, you're showing love to God too!

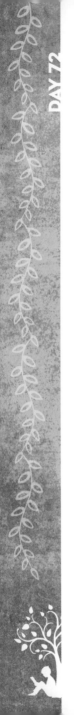

God, thank you for noticing me. Thank you for seeing
what I do when no one else does. I love you.

Wilderness Camp

John grew up and became strong in spirit.
And he lived in the wilderness until he
began his public ministry to Israel.

Luke 1:80 NLT

Have you ever wanted to go camping all summer long? John the Baptist did something like that. He went out and lived in the desert. He ate bugs and wild honey. He dressed in simple clothes. He probably even slept outside. After all of that, John was ready to do the special job God asked him to do.

Sometimes, God asks his followers to go to unusual places, just like John in the desert. Do you think God might be getting you ready for something special? It's okay if you don't know. But if he sends your family to a surprising place someday, think about the special job God may have for you.

꩜ **PRAYER** ꩜

Dear God, John the Baptist had to do some unusual things to serve
you. Please help me get ready to do the things you want me to do.

Ordinary is Extraordinary

But God has chosen the foolish things of the world to shame the wise, and God has chosen the weak things of the world to shame the things which are strong.

1 Corinthians 1:27 NASB

Do you ever feel like God only cares about people who are super strong, smart, or talented? Don't worry. God loves people who know they are weak too. And everyone has weaknesses!

Guess what—God allowed weaknesses in your life on purpose. Maybe you think God only wants to use the things that you are good at. But he wants to use your weaknesses too! The Bible is filled with stories like that. God loves to use ordinary people with regular weaknesses. With his help, they can do amazing things. And you can too! Just ask God to help you.

⁂⁂⁂ PRAYER ⁂⁂⁂

God, thank you for loving me just the way I am. I
want to do amazing things with your help!

Weak and Proud of It

But he said to me, "My grace is sufficient for you, for my power is made perfect in weakness." Therefore I will boast all the more gladly about my weaknesses, so that Christ's power may rest on me.

2 Corinthians 12:9 NIV

Did you know there is a World's Strongest Man contest? The players have to lift up super heavy logs and stones. They even bend metal pipes. For these men, weakness is a bad thing.

In the Bible, a man named Paul says weakness is a good thing. When Paul felt weak, he would remember to think more about God. And when he did that, he felt a whole lot stronger! We are no different than Paul. We can do nothing without God. But God can make us strong.

The next time you feel weak, remember that God can do anything!

⊱⊰ PRAYER ⊱⊰

God, feeling weak stinks. When I have problems, help me
remember how strong you are. You can do anything!

Tough as Nails

But I will make you as unyielding and hardened as they are. I will make your forehead like the hardest stone, harder than flint. Do not be afraid of them or terrified by them, though they are a rebellious people.

Ezekiel 3:8–9 NIV

What's the hardest thing you've ever done? Get a shot from your doctor? Say you're sorry? Clean up a mess you didn't make? Everyone has to do things that are scary or seem unfair sometimes.

God asks us to do hard things too. In the Bible, God asked a man named Ezekiel to do a really hard job. But first, he made sure Ezekiel was ready. God helped Ezekiel and made him tough and strong.

So don't worry. Whenever you have to do something really tough, remember that God will always be there to help you.

࿘ **PRAYER** ࿘

God, please help me be ready for the tough things in my life. And help me to trust you when things get hard.

Ask a Lot

Now glory be to God, who by his mighty power at work within us is able to do far more than we would ever dare to ask or even dream of—infinitely beyond our highest prayers, desires, thoughts, or hopes.

Ephesians 3:20 TLB

What do you ask God for when you pray? God dares you to ask for big things. This means that you cannot ask God for too much. You cannot dream too big. No matter what big, wild thing you think up, God can go even bigger and wilder! God says, "Trust me. Ask me anything. I can do it."

What do you want God to do in your life? You can ask him to heal an injury or sickness. You can ask him to help you solve a problem with a friend. You can ask him anything. And you can always trust that he will answer.

⚛ **PRAYER** ⚛

God, it's amazing that I can pray to you about anything! Help me remember to ask you anything that's in my heart, because you will always listen.

Feeling Forgotten

How long, LORD? Will you forget me forever?

How long will you hide your face from me?

Psalm 13:1 NIV

H ave you ever asked your mom or dad to help you with something, but they say to wait because they are busy? You wait. But after a few minutes, you go back. You're worried they might forget.

Do you ever feel that way when you pray? You ask God for help. You wait. Then you wonder why you are waiting so long. It's okay to tell God what you want. It's even okay to ask him if he has forgotten about you. The cool thing, though, is that God never, ever forgets about you or your prayers! And he always wants to hear how you feel.

God, sometimes when I wait for my prayers to be
answered I feel forgotten. Please remind me that you
are always close and listening to my every word.

Pass it On

He told them, "The secret of the kingdom of God

has been given to you. But to those on the outside

everything is said in parables . . ." Then Jesus said

to them, "Don't you understand this parable?

How then will you understand any parable?"

Mark 4:11, 13 NIV

What's your favorite way to learn? Maybe you practice reading by reading your favorite story over and over. Maybe you use flashcards to help you learn math. In Jesus' time, many people couldn't read. They didn't have TV, Internet, or iPhones. In fact, most people couldn't read. They learned by listening to people talk.

Jesus knew that telling stories was the best way to help people learn from him. He told stories that made sense to the people who lived during that time. If Jesus lived on Earth today, his stories

would probably sound very different. Jesus will do anything to help people learn about God's forgiveness, love, and guidance.

-》》》— **PRAYER** —《《《-

Jesus, I'm glad you care about helping me learn about God. I want people at school, home, church, and in my neighborhood to learn about you too. Will you show me how to help them?

Special Mission

They brought the boy to Eli. "Sir, do you remember me?"
Hannah asked. "I am the very woman who stood here
several years ago praying to the LORD. I asked the LORD
to give me this boy, and he has granted my request. Now
I am giving him to the LORD, and he will belong to the
LORD his whole life." And they worshiped the LORD there.

1 Samuel 1: 25–28 NLT

amuel was one of the bravest boys in the Bible. When Samuel was a young child, he went to live and serve God at the temple. Even though he left home, Samuel wasn't afraid to be in a new place. When he was still a child, Samuel accepted a big mission from God. One day he would become one of Israel's greatest prophets.

Can you imagine being on a mission for God? It doesn't matter if you are a child or an adult. All kinds of people can bring God's messages to the world. Maybe one day God will give you a mission too.

>))) **PRAYER** (((<

Dear God, I don't know if I'm ready for a big mission.
Will you help me get ready to do whatever you ask
me to do? I want to accept your mission.

Stand Firm

The wicked are overthrown and are no more,

but the house of the righteous stands firm.

Proverbs 12:7 NIV

Have you ever played King of the Hill? You know the game where you fight your way to the top of a pile of dirt or snow. Then, when you get to the top, you turn around and try to keep everyone else from becoming the king of the hill.

The game can be fun, but it's not fun to act that way in real life. Life is not about getting to the "top" (like being the coolest or the strongest or having the most friends), especially if that means putting other people down so you can move up.

But God sees when people become king (or queen) of the hill by pushing others around. You don't need to act like that—if you stick with the real King, Jesus, you will always be a winner.

꙳꙳꙳ **PRAYER** ꙳꙳꙳

God, being on top looks great, but I know it doesn't last for long. I want to stay on the ground and do the right thing. Help me not to push people around and remind me to pray for people who mistreat others.

No Comparisons

We won't dare compare ourselves with those who think so much of themselves. But they are foolish to compare themselves with themselves.

2 Corinthians 10:12 CEV

Can you think of a time when you compared yourself to a friend? Maybe you compared how you look, or the size of your room. God says that you shouldn't compare who you are or what you have with anyone else. Why? Because you are special beyond compare, and so is everyone else. God made each of us "one of a kind."

God doesn't want you to try to be like someone else. He just wants you to do what he created you to do. What has God given to you? How are you making the most of it?

God, you made me special, and you made everyone else special too!

Help me remember that. I don't want to compare myself to others.

Timeless

This is the interpretation, Your Majesty, and this is the decree the Most High has issued against my lord the king: You will be driven away from people and will live with the wild animals; you will eat grass like the ox and be drenched with the dew of heaven.

Daniel 4:24–25 NIV

There once was a king who had a crazy dream. So he talked to Daniel, who knew all about dreams. Daniel told the king what the dream meant. And it wasn't good news! Would you want to tell bad news to a king? Daniel had to. But Daniel was able to tell the truth in a way that wouldn't upset the king. God helped him think carefully about his words before he spoke.

Sometimes telling the truth is tricky. But God can help us, just like he helped Daniel. When we need to tell a truth, God will help us tell it in the right way.

⫸ PRAYER ⫷

God, please help me tell the truth in the right
way. I don't know if I am brave enough to do that.
Will you help me like you helped Daniel?

Okay with You

Daniel replied, "No wise man, astrologer, magician,

or wizard can tell the king such things, but there

is a God in heaven who reveals secrets …"

Daniel 2:27–28 TLB

Scientists can help us understand a lot. They can tell us why the sky is blue, or why birds fly south in the winter. But they can't explain everything. There is a lot of mysterious stuff in the world that they can only guess about. Some things only God knows!

It's easy to feel shy around people who seem smarter than you. But God doesn't care who knows the most, because he knows more than the smartest person on Earth! So instead of feeling shy, why not thank God for the way he made you?

꧁ PRAYER ꧂

Lord, I may not know much about some things, but you
know everything. And you know me! Thank you.

Who Are You Watching?

Envy can eat you up.

Proverbs 14:30 CEV

D o you sometimes look at what other kids are wearing, or what kind of toys they have? It's okay to do that. God made us to be interested in others. But do you ever start wanting other kids' stuff instead of what you have? This feeling is called envy, or jealousy.

Jealousy is like a trap. It makes you feel sad and upset. It also makes you forget about all the wonderful things God gave you, and how special he made you to be. Be thankful that God has a special plan just for you. It's good that God didn't make us all the same.

⋙ PRAYER ⋘

God, I know I get jealous sometimes. Teach me how to love those people instead of being jealous of them. Help me to be thankful for all the good things you have put in my life.

Share It

Now there were some Greeks among those who went

up to worship at the festival. They came to Philip,

who was from Bethsaida in Galilee, with a request.

"Sir," they said, "we would like to see Jesus."

John 12:20–21 NIV

When you make Jesus a big part of your life, other people will notice. It won't be a secret. Your friends will know that you pray and go to church on Sundays. That's a good thing! And if they ask you to tell them about Jesus, well, that's an even better thing.

What would you say to someone who asks you about God? You could start with something simple. You could also ask that person to come to church with you and your family. There is always room for more in God's house.

Jesus, I don't always know how to tell people about you.
Please give me the right words at the right time.

God Sees It All

Seated in a window was a young man named
Eutychus, who was sinking into a deep sleep as
Paul talked on and on. When he was sound asleep,
he fell to the ground from the third story and was
picked up dead. Paul went down, threw himself
on the young man and put his arms around him.
"Don't be alarmed," he said. "He's alive!"

Acts 20:9–10 NIV

One day, a young man named Eutychus was listening to the great teacher Paul talk about Jesus. As Paul kept talking and talking, Eutychus started feeling sleepy. Before long it was dark outside, and Eutychus fell asleep.

God didn't get mad at Eutychus for sleeping. God is our Creator, and he knows our bodies. He knows how much food we should eat, how much water we should drink, and when it's time

for us to sleep. God knows our hearts too. He saw the love in Eutychus' heart. He saw the way Eutychus listened to Paul teach about Jesus. And he saw how Eutychus stuck around, even when he could have gone home. That made God happy.

⫸ ——PRAYER—— ⫷

God, I'm so happy that you see the real me and know
what I need. I want you to be my best friend.

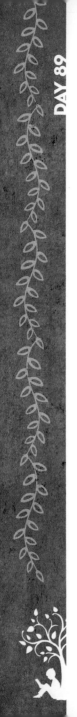

Joy Forever

I tell you, there is rejoicing in the presence of the

angels of God over one sinner who repents.

Luke 15:10 NIV

When you share the good news about Jesus, it's a wonderful thing. The most joyful day of your life is when you decide to follow Jesus. But imagine this happening in heaven: someone you told about Jesus comes over to you and says, "I want to thank you. I am here because you shared Jesus with me." Now that will be a joyful day too! And that kind of joy doesn't have to wait for heaven. It begins here on Earth when you help others join God's family.

Ask God to help you spread the Good News. It will lead to true joy.

⋙ **PRAYER** ⋘

*Jesus, I don't always feel like talking to other kids about you. Please
give me a heart full of love for people who don't know you yet.*

Keeping God in the Neighborhood

Son of man, if a country sins against me by being unfaithful and I stretch out my hand against it to cut off its food supply and send famine upon it and kill its people and their animals, even if these three men—Noah, Daniel and Job—were in it, they could save only themselves by their righteousness, declares the Sovereign LORD.

Ezekiel 14:13–14 NIV

There are lots of stories about Noah, Daniel, and Job in the Bible. These three men loved God and tried their best to please him. God says they were righteous, which means they lived the way God wanted them to live. God was so important to them.

We need more people like Noah, Daniel, and Job in our

world. Righteous people set an example of how to live a good life here on Earth. When we live righteous lives, we bring God with us wherever we go. And our words and actions can point other people to God's love and goodness.

·ঽঽ৷· **PRAYER** ·ঽ৷·

Lord, help me be a light to people around me. Let them see your love and goodness through me.

Being Kind

Isaac was forty years old when he married Rebekah

daughter of Bethuel the Aramean from Paddan

Aram and sister of Laban the Aramean.

Genesis 25:20 NIV

The Bible tells us about a woman named Rebekah. Rebekah was very brave. She helped strangers. She moved away from home when she was young. That took courage! She was generous too. She shared what she had with others who needed help.

Rebekah trusted God and treated others kindly. You can be that kind of person too. It doesn't matter how old you are or where you live. When you are kind, other kids will want to be around you. And your kindness will show others that God is kind too. That's the kind of kid God wants you to be.

-)))—**PRAYER**—(((-

God, help me to be the kind of person you want me to be.
How can I treat others better and show them your love?

Don't Give Up on the Bad Guys

All the people saw this and began to mutter, "He [Jesus] has gone to be the guest of a 'sinner.'" But Zacchaeus stood up and said to the Lord, "Look, Lord! Here and now I give half of my possessions to the poor, and if I have cheated anybody out of anything, I will pay back four times the amount."

Luke 19:7–8 NIV

Zacchaeus was the chief tax collector in Jericho, and he was able to force people to pay as much money as he wanted. Sometimes he would charge them more taxes than they owed and then he would keep that money for himself. He became rich by cheating other people.

One day Jesus came to Jericho and he insisted on having dinner with Zacchaeus. Everyone in town was shocked that Jesus would even associate with such a cheat.

But because Jesus showed kindness to Zacchaeus, the

tax collector began to change. In fact, he said he would repay
everyone he cheated four times as much as he took from them.

We all know girls and boys who don't play fair. They cheat and
don't let others have a turn. They take what's not theirs or hurt
others. We don't have to be friends with these people. But we can
still try to treat them like Jesus would. Our prayers, words, and
actions can help them see the right way to act.

PRAYER

God, sometimes I wish mean kids would just disappear.
But you created those kids. You want them to become part
of your family, just like I am. Help me show them what
you are like with my prayers, words, and actions.

God Loves Everyone the Same

There is neither Jew nor Gentile, neither
slave nor free, nor is there male and female,
for you are all one in Christ Jesus.

Galatians 3:28 NIV

When Jesus was a little boy, the men in his hometown would sometimes pray this prayer: "Lord, thank you for not making me a dog or a woman." Can you imagine being a girl back then? You would have been treated the same as your family pet. Many men were not that nice toward women. They thought they were somehow better than them, which is completely wrong.

God loves everyone the same and each person is as important as the next. But we don't always act as though it's true. This happened in the Bible, and it still happens today. Some people

make fun of kids who are different. Other people aren't always respectful to kids with special needs or who are from different cultures. What will you do to treat everyone the same and help spread kindness and respect where you live?

⋙ PRAYER ⋘

Lord, please forgive me for when I am not kind or respectful to others. I want to honor you and treat others with respect and kindness. Please help me make changes for the better.

Listening to Others

Spouting off before listening to the facts

is both shameful and foolish.

Proverbs 18:13 NLT

What's the most important thing a doctor should know before helping someone? What body part needs fixing! Can you imagine if he didn't listen to the patient or the nurse? He might put a cast on the wrong leg.

Listening is very important when you're a doctor, but it's important for the rest of us too. When we interrupt someone or don't listen to them, we're telling the other person they're not worth listening to. It can be fun to talk but try to be just as excited to hear what someone else is saying. When we treat people respectfully—looking them in the eye, smiling, and paying attention—we are doing what Jesus taught us.

⁂ PRAYER ⁂

Lord, help me say good things that bring you praise.

Teach me to listen to others like you listen to me.

Take Care

If you see your neighbor's ox or sheep or goat

wandering away, don't ignore your responsibility.

Take it back to its owner. Do the same if you find your

neighbor's donkey, clothing, or anything else your

neighbor loses. Don't ignore your responsibility.

Deuteronomy 22:1, 3 NLT

What would you do if you saw a lost cell phone at the park? You know you should try to find its owner or give it to a grown up, but you're having too much fun playing. Oh well, you think. I'm sure someone else will help!

In the Bible, God told his children to take care of each other's things and return lost items. That's because God wants us to be caring instead of selfish. And when we help people, we act like Jesus. So when you find money on the ground, a lost phone, or a missing game, turn it in or try to return it. After all, if you lost something, wouldn't you want someone to return it to you?

God, I don't always feel like doing the right thing.

Please give me a caring, selfless attitude like yours.

Help me treat others how I want to be treated.

The Golden Rule

"Love your neighbor as yourself." Love does no harm to a neighbor. Therefore love is the fulfillment of the law.

Romans 13:9–10 NIV

Gold is beautiful and worth a lot of money. Who wouldn't want something made of real gold? The Golden Rule is worth even more than gold. It says to treat others the way you want to be treated. That's the kind of gold God likes. Why? Because everyone matters to God!

Think of five things you would love for your friends or family to do for you. Surprise you with a bowl of ice cream? Share a favorite game or toy? Help you pick up your messy room? Now try doing these kinds of things for someone else.

⫸ PRAYER ⫷

Lord, please help me follow the Golden Rule. I want to treat others the way I like being treated.

Change the World

Speak up for those who cannot speak for themselves,
for the rights of all who are destitute. Speak up and
judge fairly; defend the rights of the poor and needy.

Proverbs 31:8–9 NIV

There's a way we can change the world. But how?

First, we have to learn how to be less selfish and more sharing. That can be hard! But here's a trick: think about how much you love your things. Now, think about people in the world who don't have many things of their own. Try to give that same love and attention to them instead of to your stuff.

Next, we need to know the right thing to do. God says he will help us with that if we ask. So start asking! Then talk to your parents or teachers at church. They can give you tips on how to help others.

That's how you start! Get ready to change the world for God.

···)) PRAYER ((···

Lord, can I really help change the world for you? It seems like such a big job. I want to help, though, if you want to use me.

Nobody's Perfect

Asa did what was right in the eyes of the LORD,
as his father David had done . . . Although he
did not remove the high places, Asa's heart was
fully committed to the LORD all his life.

1 Kings 15:11, 14 NIV

Who do you think would win a "World's Best Christian" contest? A missionary, a preacher, or someone else you know? We don't need a contest, because God loves all of us the same. And everyone messes up sometimes, even the "best" Christians. We don't need to be perfect to make God happy.

The Bible tells us about King Asa. He loved God all his life. But he wasn't perfect. He didn't follow all of God's rules perfectly. But God knows us inside and out. He knows we cannot be perfect.

Even when you mess up, God will never stop loving you!

⫸⫸ **PRAYER** ⫷⫷

Lord, I'm glad I don't have to be perfect.
Please help me to always do my best.

Thankful for Good News

*Let the redeemed of the L*ORD* tell their story —*

those he redeemed from the hand of the

foe, those he gathered from the lands, from

east and west, from north and south.

Psalm 107:2–3 NIV

Getting a new baby brother or sister, going on a trip, enjoying a birthday party—these things are good news! They make you happy or excited. And they make you want to tell everyone. You don't want to keep good news to yourself. What fun would that be?

Many places in the Bible tell people to share good news. But a lot of the time we see so much bad news on TV, like fires, accidents, and fighting. It can be easy to forget about all the good news.

Let's follow the example of the Bible. Let others know about the good things God gives.

⋙ PRAYER ⋘

Lord, there are so many good things in my life. But sometimes I only think about the bad stuff. Thank you for all the wonderful blessings you've given me. Help me to share them with others today and every day.

Shout it Out!

Praise the LORD. Praise God in his sanctuary;

praise him in his mighty heavens.

Psalm 150:1 NIV

You've learned about God's awesome power. You've heard about his amazing love. The Bible has told you how he saves the sick, the dying, and the hurting. He protects his children. He provided his own Son, Jesus Christ, to die for us. And he wants you to live with him in paradise.

That's worth singing and shouting about!

Think about all the things you have learned about God. Thank him for the goodness in your life, each and every day. You can trust God to help you as you grow up. He will take care of you. He is the Creator who made you and loves you forever. Praise him!

⋙ PRAYER ⋘

God, I praise you for your wonderful creations, marvelous love,
and awesome power. Thank you for bringing me into your family.

God's Big Plans for Me Storybook Bible

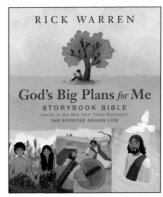

Based on the *New York Times* Bestseller
The Purpose Driven Life

By #1 *New York Times* Bestselling
Author **Rick Warren**

With child-friendly language, engaging illustrations, and a chronological approach, Pastor Warren introduces each Bible story with a theme that aligns with one of his foundational principles from *The Purpose Driven Life*. He wraps up the stories with a closing thought targeted to early readers.

Purpose Driven Life Devotional for Kids

By #1 *New York Times* Bestselling
Author **Rick Warren**

Written especially for children ages 8 and up, and featuring a ribbon marker, each of the 365 devotions includes a Scripture, short message, and prayer or thought for the day to help kids discover who they are in God's eyes. Capturing the hearts of the new generation means ensuring they know their purpose and grow up confident of their value in God and their relationship to Christ.

Available in stores and online!